The Period Comic
Hutcheon Low Drive
Aberdeen, United Kingdom

For enquiries, email:ask@theperiodcomic.com
www.theperiodcomic.com
Facebook: The period comic
Instagram: theperiodcomic

ISBN 978-1-9162810-3-5
Published by
The Period Comic, Tricia Sanitary Products,
United Kingdom

Illustrator: Epoch Studios
www.epochstudios.co

Printed in the United Kingdom

I dedicate this book to my amazing children
Ian and Tricia Igboayaka.
Love you guys.

A percentage of proceeds from this book
will be used for periodkits and products to support
girls undergoing period poverty.

EXCITING REVIEWS

"

My favourite character is Ada because she is bold and very interesting. I love this book because it's not just a fantasy, it's real and it tells a story about girls and their periods. It gives girls confidence about their bodies and takes away fear regarding periods. I recommend it to all girls over 9 and it is by far the most appropriate period book for girls. I love this book a lot and it is really the best!

Amiee 9 years old (United Kingdom)

The Period Comic is amazing, It's brilliant, it's the best! As soon as I started reading it, I could not put it down. Although the girls are from different ethnicities, they have one thing in common and that is to learn all about their bodies. This book takes away the fear of periods.
I love this book. It is a must have. I am recommending it to my friends.

Oyin 10 years old (United Kingdom)

Wow!! The period comic is amazing. It is so easy to understand. I can identify with some of the things described in the book. I particularly love the fact that is in a comic format. I love the characters in the book. I have told my friends about the book and they can't wait to get their copies.

Aj 11years old (United Kingdom)

I could not drop the period comic once I started reading it. It is interesting and engaging. I love it! Thank you for letting me read this. It is so much fun and easy to understand. I can totally relate with the illustrations.

Dee 13years (United Kingdom)

"

www.theperiodcomic.com

WHY GIRLS LOVE THE PERIOD COMIC

Easy to understand and relatable

The Period Comic explains periods (menstruation) in a practical
and easy way that young girls can relate to. It is fun filled thus eases
the anxiety and numerous questions about periods most girls have.
The story involves practical tips and has been illustrated using beautiful
characters with great personalities.

WHAT MAKES THE PERIOD COMIC AMAZING?

Medically reviewed

The period comic was reviewed by an experienced gynaecologist.

Properly researched & influenced by real life experiences

Information in this book was informed by intensive research and experience
garnered over the years of working with young girls in different communities
and documenting their experiences regarding periods.

Includes period poverty awareness

Period poverty is a global issue and many girls miss school monthly because
of lack of access to hygienic period products. Lack of awareness about periods
is also a form of poverty. This book was also influenced by the knowledge gap
about periods.

It is a must have for all girls from age 8+

www.theperiodcomic.com

THE PERIOD COMIC

PUBERTY, PERIODS & PERIOD POVERTY, A GIRL'S ULTIMATE GUIDE

Join **Ada**, **Anabel** and **Misha** as they embark on another intriguing adventure of self-discovery. Follow them on their journey as they explore their inner strengths to effect positive change in their community. They also join in teaching girls about puberty and periods.

CONNECT WITH THE PERIOD COMIC MAIN CHARACTERS

ANABEL

ANABEL IS SHY BUT IS INTUITIVE, INTELLIGENT AND GIVES GREAT ADVICE. SHE IS ALWAYS SEEKING MORE KNOWLEDGE AND WANTS TO LEARN AS MUCH AS SHE CAN ABOUT THINGS ESPECIALLY THE CHANGES IN HER BODY. SHE SOMETIMES FEELS OVERCOME BY HER DEEP THOUGHTS AND EMOTIONS. SHE LOVES WRITING.

HER FAVOURITE COLOUR IS YELLOW FOR HER. YELLOW STANDS FOR HAPPINESS AND POSITIVITY.

STRENGTH: INTELLIGENCE

CONNECT WITH THE PERIOD COMIC MAIN CHARACTERS

ADA

ADA IS BOLD, CONFIDENT AND VERY CREATIVE. SHE LOVES ADVENTURE AND LOVES TO MAKE FRIENDS. SHE'S VERY GOAL-ORIENTED AND IS ALWAYS WORKING ON A PROJECT. SHE CAN BE A PERFECTIONIST SOMETIMES. ADA IS ALWAYS UP FOR TRYING SOMETHING NEW.

FAVOURITE COLOUR IS ORANGE. FOR HER, ORANGE STANDS FOR STRENGTH, CREATIVITY AND NEW OPPORTUNITIES.

STRENGTH: CONFIDENCE

CONNECT WITH THE PERIOD COMIC MAIN CHARACTERS

MISHA:

MISHA IS VERY HOSPITABLE. LOVING, KIND AND PEACEFUL. SHE ALWAYS SEES THE GOOD IN EVERYONE AND IS ALWAYS WANTING TO HELP OTHERS. SHE LOVES VOLUNTEERING, TAKING CARE OF OTHERS, AND LOOKING FOR WAYS TO BRING MORE LOVE INTO THE WORLD. SHE CAN SEEM CAREFREE SOMETIMES.

FAVOURITE COLOUR IS PURPLE. FOR HER, PURPLE STANDS FOR ROYALTY AND SHE SEES EVERY GIRL AS A PRINCESS.

STRENGTH: COMPASSION

IT'S THE **LAST** DAY OF **SCHOOL** AND THE PUPILS ARE LOOKING **FORWARD** TO THE HOLIDAYS.

IT'S TWO WEEKS TO **ADA'S** 10TH **BIRTHDAY**.

YOU HAVE ALL BEEN **INVITED**.

DURING THE **HOLIDAYS**, OUR COMMUNITY WILL BE **ORGANISING** A CAMPAIGN TAGGED #PERIODPOVERTY.

AS **PART** OF THE CAMPAIGN, SOME OF YOUR **CLASSMATES** WILL BE HAVING A BAKE SALE IN **SUPPORT** OF THE **CAUSE**.

ADA, MISHA AND **ANABEL**, CAN YOU COME AND TELL THE **CLASS** WHAT THE **BAKE SALE** IS ABOUT?

11

WE ARE *HAVING* A BAKE SALE TO RAISE FUNDS IN *SUPPORT* OF GIRLS *EXPERIENCING* PERIOD POVERTY.

THANKS GIRLS

REMIND YOUR *PARENTS* ABOUT THE *#PERIODPOVERTY* CAMPAIGN AT THE COMMUNITY CENTRE AND *DON'T* FORGET TO PICK UP A *LEAFLET* ON *YOUR* WAY OUT.

DING! DING! DONG!

YES MISS KAREN

THAT IS *ALL* WE *HAVE* FOR TODAY. HAVE A WONDERFUL *HOLIDAY.*

THE *GIRLS* *GET UP* AND LEAVE TOGETHER CHATTING

I STILL *REMEMBER* THE AMAZING *WEEKEND* WE HAD AT YOUR *HOUSE*

YES ADA, WE HAD SO MUCH FUN. NOW I *CAN'T* WAIT FOR *TOMORROW* WHEN WE GET TO PLAN THE *BAKE* SALE.

WE'RE *GOING* TO HAVE THE BEST TIME. MY MUM HAS *SORTED* OUT OUR FOOD PERMIT AND WE'RE *GOOD* TO GO.

ARE WE STILL *MEETING* THIS EVENING TO SHARE LEAFLETS FOR THE *BAKE* SALE?

YES! I AM SO EXCITED THAT WE CAN *SUPPORT* THE PERIOD POVERTY *AWARENESS* CAMPAIGN.

CHAPTER 1

WE USE OUR TALENTS TO MAKE A DIFFERENCE

- WE LOVE OUR NEW PROJECT
- PERIOD POVERTY. WHAT'S THAT?

WHAT IS *PERIOD* POVERTY?

PERIOD POVERTY IS WHEN *SOMEONE* CANNOT AFFORD TO BUY THE *PRODUCTS* THEY NEED FOR THEIR *PERIODS*, ALSO WHEN THEY DO NOT HAVE *KNOWLEDGE* ABOUT PERIODS.

HAVE YOU *STARTED* YOUR *PERIOD* YET?

YES, I *HAVE* . . . LAST YEAR.

I NEED TO GO *BACK* INTO THE *HOUSE*. I AM HELPING MY DAD *WATCH* MY SIBLINGS.

WHAT OF YOUR *MUM?*

SHE IS WORKING. SHE *WORKS* TWO JOBS AND SHE IS *HARDLY* HOME.

IF SHE *DOSEN'T* WORK TWO *JOBS*, WE WON'T HAVE ENOUGH FOR *UPKEEP*

OH NO.

DOES YOUR DAD NOT *WORK?*

NO. HE HAD AN *ACCIDENT* SOME YEARS AGO, SO HE *CAN'T* WORK.

OH NO. *THAT'S A SHAME.*

CAN I *JOIN* YOU FOR THE BAKE SALE? I CAN ASK MY *PARENTS*.

SURE. WE WILL BE AT THE *COMMUNITY* CENTRE BY *12 NOON* ON *SATURDAY*

YOU CAN *JOIN* US FOR *MOVIES* TOO, SOMETIME

THANKS

SEE YOU *TOMORROW*

SEE YOU TOMORROW

AFTERWARDS, THEY SAY THEIR GOODBYES, HUG AND GO HOME

THE GIRLS ARE SITTING OUT IN THE *GARDEN*, *PLANNING* THEIR BAKE SALE AND WHAT THEY *INTEND* TO DO.

WOULD YOU *GIRLS* LIKE SOMETHING TO *DRINK?*

YES, *DAD.*

YES PLEASE, MR *SMITH.*

I KIND OF HAVE AN IDEA FOR HOW WE *SHOULD PLAN* THE BAKE SALE AND CHARITY EVENT.

ADA, *YOU* LOVE WORKING ON NEW *PROJECTS*

YES, I DO AND I AM SO EXCITED ABOUT THIS ONE. MY *MUM* SAYS THAT WE CAN JOIN THE TEAM TO *DISTRIBUTE* PERIOD PRODUCTS TO SOME HOMES.

I LOVE THAT. I WOULD *LOVE* TO *VOLUNTEER* FOR THE DISTRIBUTION. I JUST NEED TO *ASK* MY MUM.

HERE *SEE*, I HAVE WRITTEN *DOWN* SOME *STUFF*

THANK YOU!

I HAVE MADE A *LIST* OF WHAT WE NEED TO DO ON THE *DAY* OF THE BAKE SALE. *AMONG* OURSELVES.

NOW WE NEED TO *SHARE* THE RESPONSIBILITIES

I HAVE AN *IDEA* TOO

I WROTE A *POEM* SOME *DAYS* AGO AND I THINK IT WOULD BE *LOVELY* TO READ IT AT THE *BAKE SALE.*

THAT'S *GOOD*, LET'S *HEAR* IT

ADA AND *MISHA'S*
MUMS TAKE THE GIRLS
OUT FOR *SHOPPING* IN
PREPARATION *FOR*
THEIR *BAKE* SALE.

CHAPTER 2

OOPS! I JUST GOT MY PERIOD

- DO CRAMPS HURT?
- HOW CAN I MANAGE CRAMPS?
- TRACK YOUR PERIODS

THE GIRLS MEET UP AT *ANABEL'S* TO *BAKE* THE *TRIAL CAKES.*

I DON'T *FEEL* WELL. MY *STOMACH* HURTS

YOU'RE *OKAY* TO THE TOUCH BUT COME WITH ME AND I'LL *CHECK* YOUR TEMPERATURE.

I'LL ALSO *CALL YOUR* MUM TO *PICK* YOU UP.

ADA, YOUR *MUM* IS HERE

THANK YOU FOR *HAVING* HER

BYE, ADA

BYE

HOW DO *YOU* FEEL?

MY STOMACH IS IN *KNOTS*, MUM. I'M *NOT SURE* WHAT IT IS.

IT'S ALRIGHT, ADA. I'LL TAKE A *BETTER* LOOK ONCE WE GET *HOME*.

MRS *ADAMS* IS A PAEDIATRICIAN (A DOCTOR WHO TREATS CHILDREN) SHE ALSO *VOLUNTEERS* WITH A *CHARITY* THAT WORKS TO ERADICATE PERIOD POVERTY IN THE COMMUNITY).

AT HOME.

WELCOME MUM. ADA YOU *DON'T* LOOK SO GOOD

YOUR *SISTER* IS *NOT* FEELING TOO WELL. WHERE IS YOUR *DAD*?

HE IS *TAKING* A *NAP*.

25

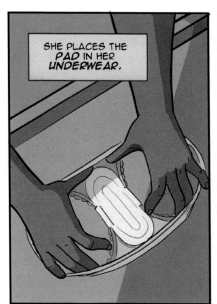

SHE PLACES THE *PAD* IN HER *UNDERWEAR.*

MUM, I *JUST* GOT MY PERIOD.

OH. REALLY? *THAT'S* GREAT.

HOW DO YOU *FEEL?* HAVE YOU *CHANGED* INTO SOME *CLEAN* UNDERWEAR?

YES MUM, I *JUST* DID. I AM SO *HAPPY* THAT YOU *TAUGHT* US ALL ABOUT *PERIODS.* I JUST USED THE SUPPLIES IN MY *STARTER* PACK.*

*(REFER TO SERIES 1)

MY *STOMACH* STILL HURTS

NOT TO *WORRY,* YOU WILL *FEEL* BETTER SOON. I WILL GET SOME *WARM* WATER IN THE HOT WATER *BOTTLE;* IT WILL *HELP* WITH THE CRAMPS.

LIE DOWN, I WILL *BACK* SHORTLY.

MRS ADAMS *RETURNS* AND *HELPS* ADA TO PLACE A HOT WATER *BOTTLE* ON HER *TUMMY*.

MUM, *HOW* LONG WILL THE *CRAMPS* LAST?

DURATION OF CRAMPING IS *DIFFERENT* FOR EVERY GIRL OR WOMAN.

SOME GIRLS DON'T GET PERIOD *CRAMPS* AT ALL, LIKE YOUR SISTER, *ZARA*.

CRAMPING STARTS *BEFORE* PERIOD AND *CONTINUES* DURING *PERIODS* FOR SOME. FOR OTHERS, IT LASTS JUST FOR A FEW DAYS OR *HOURS*.

OH *NO*. I HOPE MINE *STOPS* NOW

DON'T *WORRY*, ALL YOU NEED DO IS TO *GET* SOME *REST*.

DOES THAT MEAN I HAVE TO *SLEEP* FOR 9 HOURS?

REMEMBER WHAT I *TAUGHT* YOU *ABOUT* RESTING?

IT *HELPS* YOUR BODY *REJUVENATE* AND REBUILD ITSELF.

32

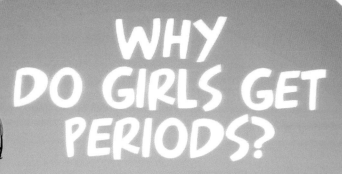

CHAPTER 3

WHY DO GIRLS GET PERIODS?

- IS IT PUBERTY YET?
- MANAGING PERIODS & PERIOD HYGIE[
- TRACK YOUR PERIODS
- PMS. WHAT'S THAT?

INSIDE THE *COMMUNITY CENTER*, MRS ADAMS EDUCATES GIRLS ABOUT *PERIODS.*

I WILL BE TALKING TO YOU ABOUT *PERIODS* (MENSTRUATION) AND SELF -*HYGIENE* DURING PERIODS

WHY DO WE *GET* PERIODS?

GIRLS GET PERIODS AS PART OF THE *PROCESS* OF GROWING UP. PERIODS COME *DURING* PUBERTY.

PUBERTY IS A *STAGE* IN THE LIFE OF *EVERY* GIRL AS THEY TRANSITION *TOWARDS* ADULTHOOD.*

*REFER TO SERIES 1

DURING THIS STAGE OF GROWTH, *HORMONES* IN YOUR BODY MAKE CHANGES TO YOUR *BODY*

WHAT *ARE* HORMONES?

THESE MESSAGES CAUSE *PHYSICAL* AND *EMOTIONAL* CHANGES TO YOUR *BODY*, INCLUDING GROWTH.

HORMONES ARE CHEMICAL MESSAGES SENT TO *DIFFERENT* PARTS OF YOUR BODY *TELLING* YOUR BODY WHAT TO DO.

WHAT *KIND* OF CHANGES?

DURING PUBERTY, YOU HAVE BOTH *PHYSICAL* AND *EMOTIONAL* CHANGES. GIRLS GROW RAPIDLY, USUALLY *FASTER* THAN BOYS OF THE SAME *AGE.*

DURING THIS TIME, GIRLS' BREASTS BEGIN TO *DEVELOP.* THIS IS *NORMAL* AND NOTHING TO *WORRY* ABOUT.

AGE 8   AGE 11   AGE 12   AGE 14   AGE 18

SOME GIRLS *BEGIN* TO *BREAK* OUT IN ACNE

AT WHAT **AGE** DOES PUBERTY START?

PUBERTY **TYPICALLY** STARTS FROM AGE 8 FOR GIRLS BUT GENERALLY **FROM** 9-14 AND AROUND 10-16 FOR **BOYS.**

WE ARE GOING TO TAKE A LITTLE **BREAK** NOW AND WHEN YOU GET BACK, I WILL BE **TELLING** YOU ALL ABOUT PERIODS.

OUTDOOR AT THE EXHIBITION STANDS AREA, THE GIRLS ARE IN GROUPS **CHATTING** AND HAVING CUPS OF DRINKS AND SOME **SNACKS.**

GIRLS ARE BACK AND *SEATED.*

PART OF PUBERTY IS *GETTING* YOUR *PERIODS.* THIS MEANS THAT YOU ARE BECOMING A *WOMAN.*

BUT I AM STILL A GIRL. HOW CAN *PERIODS* MAKE ME A *WOMAN?*

NO, THIS DOES *NOT* MEAN YOU ARE A WOMAN JUST YET. BUT YOUR *BODY* NEEDS TO *PREPARE* FOR WHEN YOU HAVE A BABY SOMEDAY, SOMETIME IN THE *FUTURE.*

PERIODS ARE *PART* OF YOUR MENSTRUAL *CYCLE.*

WHAT IS *MENSTRUAL* CYCLE?

MENSTRUAL CYCLE IS THE HORMONAL *PROCESS* A WOMAN'S *BODY* GOES THROUGH EACH MONTH TO PREPARE FOR A POSSIBLE *PREGNANCY.*

ITS DURATION IS TYPICALLY 28 DAYS BUT *MAY* ALSO LAST 21-35 *DAYS.* GIRLS HAVE PERIODS DURING THE *MENSTRUAL* CYCLE.

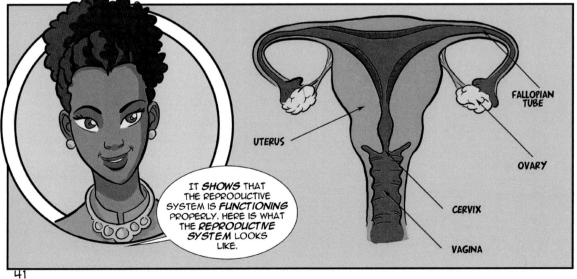

IT *SHOWS* THAT THE REPRODUCTIVE SYSTEM IS *FUNCTIONING* PROPERLY. HERE IS WHAT THE *REPRODUCTIVE SYSTEM* LOOKS LIKE.

FALLOPIAN TUBE

UTERUS

OVARY

CERVIX

VAGINA

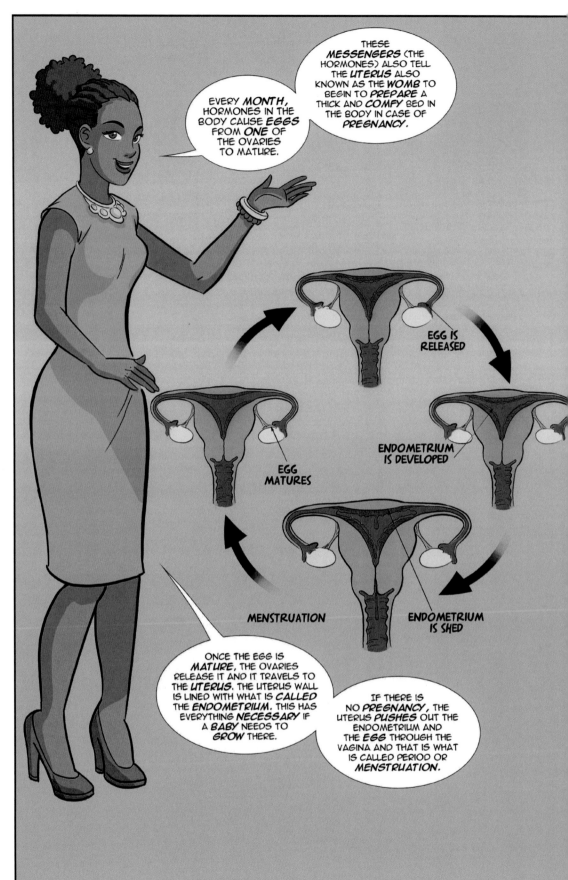

43

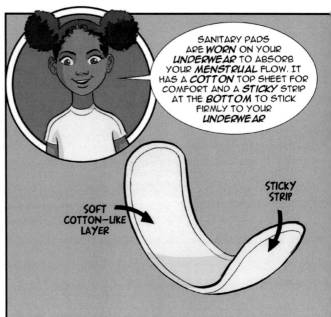

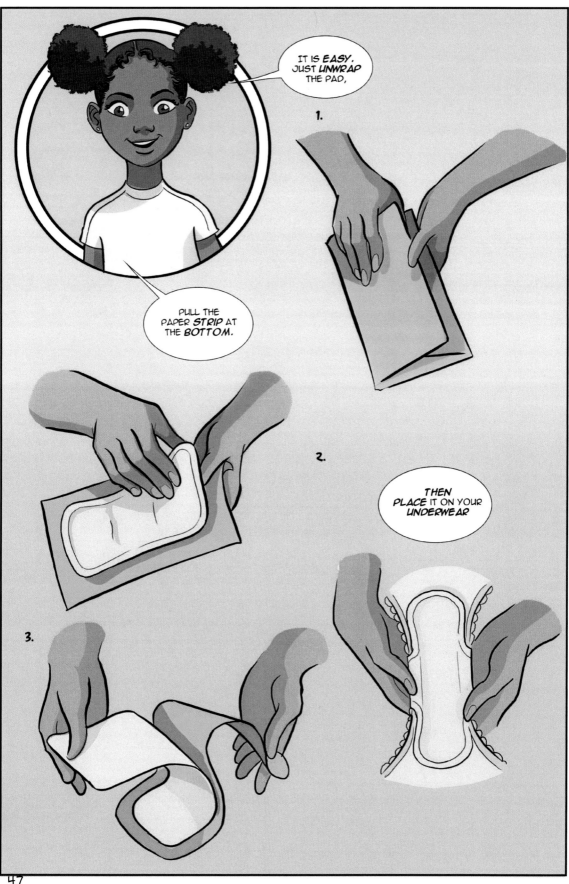

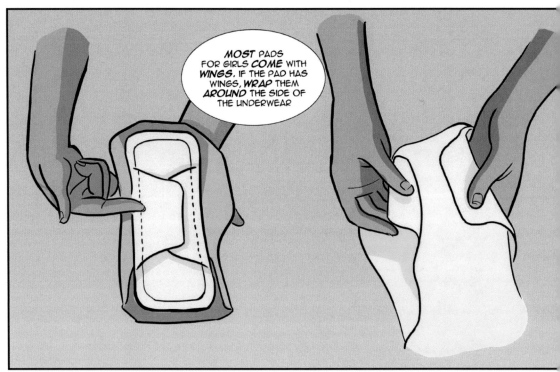

MOST PADS FOR GIRLS COME WITH WINGS. IF THE PAD HAS WINGS, WRAP THEM AROUND THE SIDE OF THE UNDERWEAR

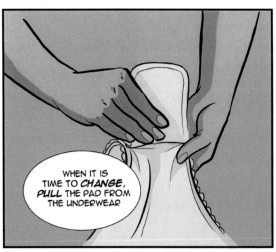

WHEN IT IS TIME TO CHANGE, PULL THE PAD FROM THE UNDERWEAR

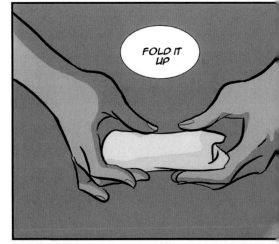

FOLD IT UP

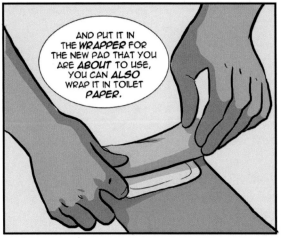

AND PUT IT IN THE WRAPPER FOR THE NEW PAD THAT YOU ARE ABOUT TO USE, YOU CAN ALSO WRAP IT IN TOILET PAPER.

AFTER WRAPPING IT, THROW IT IN A BIN. YOU CAN FIND BINS IN TOILETS. SOME FEMALE TOILETS HAVE SPECIAL BINS FOR SANITARY PRODUCTS.

CHAPTER 4

WE LOVE SERVING OUR COMMUNITY

- TOGETHER, WE CAN MAKE A DIFFEREN
- WE LOVE HAVING FUN TOO
- CAMPAIGN AGAINST PERIOD POVERTY
- WOW! WE JUST GOT REWARDED

EAT LOTS OF *FRUITS* AND *VEGETABLES* DURING YOUR PERIOD TO *HELP* YOUR *IRON* LEVEL.

HAVING 5 A DAY IN YOUR *MEAL* IS ESSENTIAL FOR *GOOD* HEALTH AND *GROWTH* *

* REFER TO SERIES 1

EXERCISE AS WELL AND YOU NEED TO SLEEP WELL. AT *LEAST* *9* HOURS DAILY

CAN I *EXERCISE* *DURING* MY PERIODS?

YES, YOU CAN. IT *HELPS* WITH CRAMPS

THANK YOU ADA

THANK YOU ADA, THAT WAS BRILLIANT.

CLAP! CLAP! CLAP!

YOU ARE WELCOME

HOW WILL I KNOW WHEN I WILL GET MY PERIOD?

NO ONE KNOWS WHEN THEY GET THEIR FIRST PERIOD, BUT YOU MAY HAVE SOME SIGNS BEFORE IT COMES.

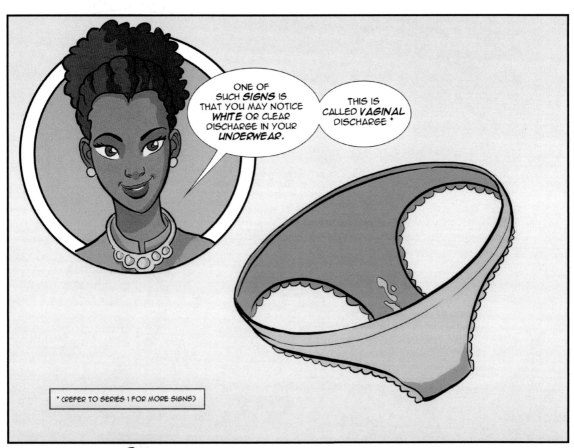

* (REFER TO SERIES 1 FOR MORE SIGNS)

THE PURSE CAN CONTAIN IMPORTANT *ITEMS* SUCH AS A PAD, *UNDERWEAR*, PANTY LINER AND *WIPES*

I *SEE* WE HAVE PERIOD *PRODUCTS* SUCH AS PADS, *TAMPONS* IN THE *TOILET* AT *SCHOOL*.

YES, *SOME* SCHOOLS AND PUBLIC PLACES HAVE *PROVIDED* PERIOD *PRODUCTS* FOR *USE* IN THEIR *TOILETS*. YOU CAN USE THEM

MY OLDER SISTER *CRAVES* FOR *SWEETS* WHEN *SHE* IS ON HER PERIOD. IS THAT *NORMAL?*

IF YOU *CRAVE* SWEETS, YOU *CAN* HAVE SOME *DARK* CHOCOLATES.

YES, *YOU* CAN GET *CRAVINGS* EVEN FOR *SWEETS*, BUT IT IS *HEALTHIER* TO TAKE FRUITS, *VEGETABLES* AND *LOTS OF WATER*.

ANABEL HAS *SOMETHING* TO *READ* TO US. ANABEL

MY *POEM* IS TITLED 'THE *STRENGTH WITHIN*'

The Strength Within.

Self-confidence is key and to help yourself, start using
it when you are young like me
You will start to believe that you are someone that
nobody else can be
You can be a beaming light or a strong and fierce knight
Just remember no one can stop you from using all of your might
If you get an answer incorrect do not hide or feel shy
You may make mistakes, but always take a lesson from them
keep in mind, that is what makes you great
Don't look back, keep moving forward.
Remember to always be yourself and try not to feel
intimidated by anyone
Be kind and loving to you, you are unique
You are a star, so let everybody know you are
Continue to challenge yourself, you are brave and bold
If you believe in yourself, you are most likely to do great things
The world will be a better place because you make an
amazing difference in it
Then you begin to inspire everyone around you
That is your power, that is the strength within.

* THIS WAS WRITTEN BY *MAY ENOW*
A 10-YEAR-OLD FROM *CAMBRIDGESHIRE,*
UNITED KINGDOM.

PMS STANDS FOR PREMENSTRUAL *SYNDROME*

PMS IS *CAUSED* BY CHANGING HORMONE *LEVELS* IN THE *BODY*.

IT IS USED TO *DESCRIBE* THE *SYMPTOMS* SOME GIRLS FEEL A FEW DAYS OR A *WEEK* TO THEIR PERIODS

THE SYMPTOMS CAN BE *PHYSICAL* AND *EMOTIONAL*. NOT EVERY GIRL WILL *EXPERIENCE* PMS.

THESE *SYMPTOMS CAN INCLUDE* MOODINESS, *BACKACHE*, *ANXIETY*, DIFFICULTY CONCENTRATING OR *EVEN* SADNESS

BLOATING OR *ACNE*.

THESE *SYMPTOMS* GO AWAY *AFTER* THE FIRST *FEW* DAYS OF A PERIOD.

IT IS GOOD TO KEEP A *JOURNAL* OF HOW YOU *FEEL* DURING PERIODS. SO THAT YOU CAN TELL AN *ADULT* IF YOU HAVE REALLY *BAD* SYMPTOMS AND YOU CAN SEE A *DOCTOR*

DO WE HAVE TO *VISIT* THE *DOCTOR* EVERY *TIME* WE GET PERIODS?.

NO, *NOT* AT ALL. YOU DON'T *HAVE* TO BE *WORRIED* ABOUT *PERIODS*.

GETTING YOUR *PERIODS* IS A GOOD THING. IT IS NOTHING TO BE *ASHAMED* OR *AFRAID* OF. IT JUST MEANS THAT YOU ARE *GROWING* UP

WITH A *JOURNAL*, YOU CAN *WRITE* DOWN YOUR *SYMPTOMS* *DURING* YOUR *PERIODS*

MY YOUNGER SISTER GOT HER *PERIOD* *BEFORE* ME. WHY IS THAT?

NO *ONE* CAN TELL. *EACH* BODY IS *UNIQUE* AND ON ITS OWN SCHEDULE, USUALLY *PERIODS* COME LIKE A YEAR OR *TWO* AFTER THE *BREASTS* BEGIN TO DEVELOP.

SOME *GIRLS* GET THEIR *PERIODS* *EARLIER* THAN OTHERS. SOME *GET* THEM AS EARLY AS 8 OR 9 *YEARS*, WHILE OTHERS *DON'T* GET THEIRS UNTIL THEY ARE 14.

IF A GIRL IS UP TO 16 YEARS OR MORE AND STILL HASN'T HAD HER FIRST PERIOD. THEN SHE SHOULD SEE A DOCTOR

DOES THAT *MEAN* SHE IS *UNWELL*?

NOT *NECESSARILY*. THE DOCTORS WILL *EXAMINE* HER TO *KNOW* WHAT TO *DO*

IF A *GIRL* IS UP *14 YEARS* OR *OLDER* AND HASN'T *EXPERIENCED* ANY SIGNS OF PUBERTY YET, SHE *SHOULD* SEE A DOCTOR.

WILL *EVERY* GIRL GET HER PERIOD EVERY *MONTH*?

AFTER YOU GET YOUR *FIRST* PERIOD, YOUR PERIOD *MIGHT* NOT BE *REGULAR* FOR A WHILE. IT COULD TAKE A *YEAR* OR TWO FOR YOUR *BODY* TO *SETTLE* INTO A REGULAR CYCLE

ONCE THE BODY HAS *SETTLED* INTO A *REGULAR* CYCLE, PERIODS HAPPEN LIKE *CLOCKWORK*. *NORMAL* PERIODS HAPPEN ONCE EVERY *MONTH* OR ONCE *EVERY* 28 DAYS *DEPENDING* ON YOUR *CYCLE*

THE GIRLS **HELP** TO **TIDY** UP THE COMMUNITY **CENTER**

TRIP TO DISTRIBUTE PERIOD PRODUCTS (THERE IS LOVE IN SHARING) #campaignagainstperiodpoverty.

THE GIRLS *JOIN* MRS *ADAMS* AND TWO OTHER MEMBERS OF HER TEAM TO *DISTRIBUTE* PERIOD *PACKS.*

WE ARE *FROM* THE *PERIOD* PLACE AND WE *HAVE* A *GIFT* FOR *YOU*

THANK YOU

WE WILL BE HEADING *OVER* TO THE COMMUNITY *CENTER* TO HAND OVER THE REMAINING *BOXES*

YOU *HAVE* DONE AN *AMAZING JOB* TODAY. *THANK* YOU

YOU ARE WELCOME

THANK YOU *MUM FOR* HAVING US

WE *LOVE* VOLUNTEERING. CAN WE *JOIN* YOU *NEXT* TIME?

SURE. ONCE YOU *GET* YOUR *PARENTS'* CONSENT.

WE WILL

THE GIRLS ARE AT *ASSEMBLY*. THE HEAD TEACHER, MRS *ROBERTS*, MAKES AN ANNOUNCEMENT.

WELCOME BACK FROM YOUR *HOLIDAYS*. I HOPE *YOU* ALL HAD AN *AMAZING* TIME.

I'M PLEASED TO *ANNOUNCE* THAT THREE *GIRLS* FROM THIS *SCHOOL* WERE *NOMINATED* FOR THE 'YOUNG *COMMUNITY* HEROES *AWARDS*'

ANABEL, *ADA* AND *MISHA* CAN YOU *PLEASE* *COME* FORWARD

THEIR INITIATIVE HAS *HELPED* THIS *COMMUNITY* RAISE FUNDS TO *SUPPORT* GIRLS *EXPERIENCING* PERIOD POVERTY

CLAP! CLAP! **CLAP!** CLAP! CLAP!

WE HAVE ALL BEEN *INVITED* BY THE *MAYOR* TO ATTEND THE AWARD *CEREMONY* ON *SATURDAY* BY 2PM.

YOUR *TEACHERS* WILL HAND OUT THE *INVITATION* LETTERS IN YOUR VARIOUS *CLASSES*.

CONGRA-TULATIONS, GIRLS!

THANK YOU!

WHICH OF THE CHARACTERS DO YOU THINK YOU ARE MOST LIKE?

ADA
STRENGTH: CONFIDENCE

ANABEL
STRENGTH: INTELLIGENCE

MISHA
STRENGTH: COMPASSION

TICK YOUR FAVOURITE CHARACTER IN THE PERIOD COMIC.

YOUR NAME...

AGE...

YOUR FAVOURITE COLOUR...

CIRCLE THE WORDS THAT BEST DESCRIBE YOU?

CARING, INTUITIVE, CHEERFUL, PLAYFUL, INTELLIGENT, INQUISITIVE, BOLD, CONFIDENT, PEACEFUL, HOSPITABLE, DRIVEN, PASSIONATE, CREATIVE, SMART, KIND, ADVENTUROUS, QUIET, COMPASSIONATE, GOAL-ORIENTED, SUPPORTIVE, SHY, LISTENER, PATIENT, HELPFUL, CHATTY, FRIENDLY.

THANK YOU!

I want to firstly acknowledge and thank **God**, my Father for the inspiration to write this book and for the grace to make a difference in so many lives. To lend my voice in promoting the education about periods in this creative way that blesses lives and liberates girls.

Special thanks to my husband *(Solomon Igboayaka)* for many nights of making this dream come through. I can't thank you enough for believing in me and being my best cheerleader.

To my family both the **Iroanyas** and the Igboayakas, I could not have asked for a better family. Special shout out to my sisters & brother- Mary, Martha and Pst. Ugo for the reviews and feedback, artwork and logo designs.

To all my friends and family who reviewed this book at one time or another, you are beyond amazing and I say a big thank you. I could not have done this without you. To all the young girls who reviewed this comic, I say thank you. Your feedback helped shape this.

My illustrator (**Martin Okonkwo** of **Epoch Comics**), thank you for bringing my imagination to life.

To the amazing **Limitless team**, who supported the campaign for this book launch, Thank you.

To all the girls I worked with who shared their period experiences with me, I say you are the best.

And **you,** yes **you.** Thanks for purchasing this book and taking the time to read it.

A GIFT FOR YOU FROM US AT THE PERIOD COMIC

FREE GIFT

To say thank you for buying my book, I have some gifts for you.

1. You can download our FREE PeriodTracker on Google play. 'Tricia Period Tracker'
2. We have a variety of free gifts for you as well.

**. Branded Positive Affirmation Posters that you can download for your wall
. Branded Confidence Wristbands
. Branded Phone Finger Holders**

Sign up and win one of our free gifts branded with The Period Comic Characters.

SCAN ME

Or visit www.theperiodcomic.com to sign up

THE PERIOD COMIC

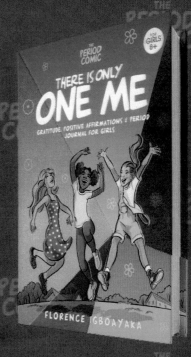

The Period Comic #1/ 2 | The Period Comic Positive Affirmation and Period Journal

ADVENTURES WITH THE PERIOD COMIC.

We are happy to announce that there are more titles in The Period Comic series. Join Ada, Anabel and Misha as they embark on more adventures of self-discovery and learning about changes happening in their bodies. Through journaling, they share exciting and fun filled experiences that more girls can enjoy and learn from. The sequel can now be purchased on the biggest global selling platform from comics and graphic novels. #Comixology and Amazon.

NOW AVAILABLE ON

comiXology an amazon company   **amazon**

f theperiodcomic   @theperiodcomic

w w w . t h e p e r i o d c o m i c . c o m

Made in the USA
Las Vegas, NV
03 December 2021